AIR
DISASTERS

Roger Coote

Thomson Learning

New York

BOOKS IN THIS SERIES

AIR DISASTERS

ENVIRONMENTAL DISASTERS

NATURAL DISASTERS

SEA DISASTERS

Cover photographs:
(Background) The wreckage of the British Midland Airways
Boeing 737 that crashed near a highway on January 8, 1989.
(Inset) One of the airplanes in the Italian Air Force aerobatic
team that crashed at the Ramstein Air Show in Germany on
August 28, 1988.

First published in the
United States in 1993 by
Thomson Learning
115 Fifth Avenue
New York, NY 10003

First published in 1993 by
Wayland (Publishers) Ltd.

Cataloging-in-Publication Data applied for

ISBN 1-56847-083-5

Printed in Italy

CONTENTS

THE SKY'S THE LIMIT

Although the aircraft is an invention of the twentieth century, the first flight by a human was made 120 years before the first powered airplane took to the air. The earliest craft was a hot-air balloon built in France by the Montgolfier brothers in 1783.

Winged airplanes developed from kites, which were flown in China as long ago as 400 B.C., but did not reach Europe until the sixteenth century. Between A.D. 1804 and 1853, an Englishman called George Cayley designed a kitelike craft called a glider—in time he built one that could carry a person.

From 1891 to 1896, the German engineer Otto Lilienthal experimented with glider designs. He made great advances in the young science of aerodynamics. However, Lilienthal died after a glider crash in 1896. He was the first victim of pilot error.

News of Lilienthal's work inspired two American brothers, Wilbur and Orville Wright, to build a machine capable of powered flight. The result was *Flyer I*, which was similar to Lilienthal's manned glider but with the addition of an engine driving two propellers. On December 17, 1903, at Kitty Hawk, North Carolina, Orville Wright made the world's first powered, controlled flight.

LEFT *Otto Lilienthal flying one of his first gliders in 1895.*

OPPOSITE *Louis Blériot became the first person to fly across the English Channel in a powered aircraft on July 25, 1909.*

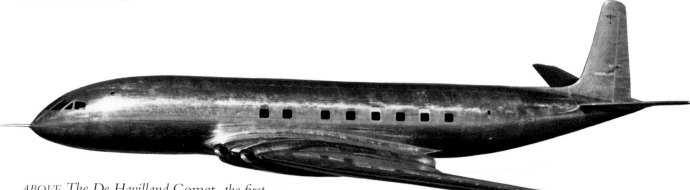

ABOVE The De Havilland Comet, *the first commercial jet airline, in 1949.*

The Wright brothers' aircraft was a biplane; that is, it had two sets of wings with one pair mounted above the other. Later the monoplane, which had one set of wings, was developed. In 1909 Frenchman Louis Blériot, used a monoplane to become the first person to fly across the English Channel. These early airplanes were constructed from wooden frames with fabric stretched over them. In 1915 the German designer Hugo Junkers started building airplanes entirely out of metal.

Since then many developments step-by-step have brought about the large, high-speed airliners and powerful military aircraft we know today. The greatest single advance was the invention of the jet engine. This engine was developed independently by both Germany and Britain in the late 1930s and early 1940s.

The world's first jet airliner, the De Havilland *Comet*, made its maiden (first) flight in 1949. Since then, passenger aircraft have become larger, faster, and safer. The first Boeing 747—called the jumbo jet —was built in 1970. It could carry 390 passengers; today's version is as tall as a six-story building and can carry more than 500 people.

Since the early days of flying, the types of accidents that happen most often have changed. At first, airplanes were fairly flimsy and unreliable, so mechanical failure was a frequent cause of accidents. Before the introduction of aircraft with pressurized cabins in 1937, airplanes had to fly at low altitudes. This meant that they were affected by bad weather more than modern airplanes.

Over the years, aircraft have become much safer and serious mechanical failures are now uncommon; they make up only 8.5 percent of all crashes, while weather conditions account for 4.5 percent. In contrast, more than 80 percent are caused by human error.

ACCIDENT CAUSES
The causes of air accidents have been calculated in percentages as follows:

- Human error   80.5%
- Mechanical failure   8.5%
- Sabotage   6.5%
- Weather   4.5%

Although aircraft have become more reliable, the number of crashes has risen steadily. This is because as air travel has become more common over the last forty years and the number of airplanes in use has grown. The size of aircraft has also increased, which means that when an accident happens involving a passenger airliner many more people could be killed.

Even so, flying keeps getting safer. Taking into account the total number of miles traveled by passengers in any year, a person is less likely to die in an airplane crash than in a train, ship, or road accident. It has been calculated that an air traveler would have to make 84,500 separate flights before he or she would be likely to be involved in an accident.

ABOVE *The horrific scene of destruction on October 4, 1992, after an El Al 747 cargo airplane crashed into an appartment complex in Amsterdam, the Netherlands.*

INSERT *The airplane had lost two of its engines after taking off from Schiphol Airport, Amsterdam. It left a path of burning fuel on the ground before it crashed.*

AIRSHIP DISASTER

On November 12, 1783, a hot-air balloon built by the brothers Joseph and Etienne Montgolfier became the first aircraft to carry people. The balloon was a magnificent craft made from blue and gold silk. It took off from the Bois de Boulogne near Paris, France, and came down to earth near the center of Paris 25 minutes later, having traveled a distance of five miles. Its two passengers, Jean Pilâtre de Rozier and the Marquis d'Arlandes, had volunteered for this history-making flight.

The air inside the Montgolfier brothers' craft was heated by burning straw and wool under the opening of the balloon. However, ten days after this first balloon flight, two people took to the air in a balloon built by Jacques Charles. It was filled with hydrogen gas, which is lighter than air and does not need to be heated.

BELOW *The Montgolfier brothers' hot-air balloon takes to the air on November 21, 1783.*

THE FIRST FATAL FLIGHT
Jean Pilâtre de Rozier, one of the passengers on the world's first balloon flight, went on to make history in another, less fortunate way. On June 15, 1785, while attempting to fly across the English Channel, his balloon caught fire and crashed. De Rozier became the first person to be killed in an aviation accident.

The main problem with the hot-air and the hydrogen balloons was that they could only go where the wind took them. This problem was solved 69 years later by Henri Giffard. He built a cigar-shaped hydrogen balloon with a platform beneath it. On the platform, he mounted a small steam engine that turned a propeller. On September 24, 1852, this airship became the first

mechanically powered craft to take to the air when Giffard piloted it on a flight of 17 miles near Paris.

Giffard's airship was too heavy to be a practical means of transporting passengers. However, with the invention of the gasoline engine and the development of aluminum (a lightweight metal) in the 1880s, airships could be made lighter and able to carry greater loads. Engineers also discovered that an airship's lifting power could be increased by making the craft longer and so capable of holding more gas.

In 1900 a German army officer, Count Ferdinand von Zeppelin, put all of these ideas together and created a long, rigid-framed airship, which was named after him. Ten years later, after several improvements

TOP *The* Graf Zeppelin, *one of the airships named after their inventor, Count Ferdinand von Zeppelin.*

ABOVE *The wreckage of the airship* R101 *after its crash in France on October 5, 1930.*

had been made, a Zeppelin service began carrying passengers in Germany. During World War I (1914-18), Zeppelins were used to carry out the first-ever air raids when they dropped bombs on London.

Following World War I, airships became fashionable as a means of transportation. By the 1930s, huge craft more than 790 feet long were being built in Germany and the United States to fly across the Atlantic Ocean. Despite their enormous size, these airships could carry only a few dozen passengers. Known as "flying hotels," they were very luxurious, and passengers had to be wealthy to afford the high fares. Between 1900 and 1939, airships carried 52,000 people on journeys totaling 1.24 million miles.

When airship accidents happened, they usually killed everybody on board. In 1930, the British airship *R101* crashed over France on its maiden flight from England to India. The 48 people on board died. Seven years later, another disaster happened, at the end of a flight from Germany to the United States by the world's largest and most luxurious airship, the *Hindenburg*.

THE *HINDENBURG*

- Built 1936.
- 812 feet long.
- 261, 611 cubic yards of gas.
- Powered by four 1,050 hp engines.

- Passenger fare was $720.
- Accommodation included large dining, lounge, smoking, and writing rooms. The cabins had sinks with hot and cold water.

LEFT In less than a minute, flames destroyed the Hindenburg.

BELOW Two survivors are helped away from the wreckage of the Hindenburg.

THE *HINDENBURG* TRAGEDY

On the evening of May 6, 1937, the *Hindenburg* came in to land at Lakehurst, New Jersey after a flight from Germany. Its arrival had been delayed by thunderstorms around New York. As the huge craft backed slowly towards its mooring mast, crew members heard a sound like gunfire. In a few seconds, the rear of the *Hindenburg* was engulfed in flames, and the airship began to crash to the ground. Passengers and crew jumped for their lives; their screams were heard by hundreds of people. Within 32 seconds, flames destroyed the whole craft, leaving only the buckled metal frame. In the end, 20 crew members, 15 passengers, and 1 member of the ground staff were killed.

No one knows what caused the disaster. The official report said that the hydrogen inside the airship was set on fire by a spark of static electricity, which had built up on the craft during the earlier thunderstorms. Some of the ground staff thought that one of the *Hindenburg*'s engines had caused a spark. Another theory is that the explosion was caused by a bomb that had been planted on board as an act of sabotage.

One definitely known thing is that the *Hindenburg* was not designed to be filled with hydrogen. It was meant to carry helium, which, unlike hydrogen, does not burn. Most helium was made in the United States.

The United States government would not allow Germany to have helium, fearing it would be used for military purposes, and so the *Hindenburg* had to use hydrogen instead. If the airship had contained helium it would not have exploded.

In the early years of aviation, it was thought that airships were more suitable for carrying passengers than winged aircraft. Airships were much quieter and allowed passengers more space and comfort. However, following the *Hindenburg* tragedy, people lost faith in airships, and engineers turned their attention to building larger, more reliable winged aircraft.

— WITNESS REPORT —

LIVE RADIO BROADCAST

Herb Morrison, a reporter from the radio station WLS, was at Lakehurst to describe for listeners the arrival of the *Hindenburg*. He began his live broadcast not knowing that disaster was about to strike.

Here it comes, ladies and gentlemen, and what a sight it is, a thrilling one, a marvelous sight …The sun is striking the windows of the observation deck on the westward side and sparkling like glittering jewels on the background of black velvet…Oh, oh, oh! …It's burst into flames…Get out of my way please, oh my this is terrible, oh my, get out of the way please! It is burning, bursting into flames and is falling…Oh! This is one of the worst…Oh! It's a terrible sight …Oh! And all the humanity…

Source: *Disasters* by Tim Healey (published by Purnell, 1988)

THE EVENING SUN

30 KILLED; CAPTAIN MAY DIE; SURVIVORS TELL OF ESCAPES

WIREPHOTO—*Hindenburg Survivor Runs For Life Out Of Flaming Wreck*

ABOVE A report of the Hindenburg *tragedy in* The Evening Sun, *a Baltimore newspaper.*

DISASTER – BY HUMAN ERROR

Looking at the sophisticated passenger jets and military aircraft of today, it is hard to believe that the first-ever flight in a powered airplane happened only 90 years ago. The design, technology, and manufacture of aircraft has improved very quickly since then, especially during the last 20 years with the development of computers. As a result, only a small percentage of aviation accidents are caused by technical failures. In contrast, mistakes by humans—including pilots, navigators, maintenance engineers, and air-traffic controllers—are estimated to account for over 80 percent of accidents.

ABOVE Part of the wrecked American Airlines DC-10, which crashed on May 25, 1979, killing all 272 people on board. The crash occurred shortly after takeoff from O'Hare International Airport in Chicago.

MAINTENANCE ERRORS

Modern aircraft are very complex machines, and it is important that they be maintained to the highest standards. They must be checked frequently and repaired when necessary. If this does not happen, the chances of a dangerous mechanical failure increase dramatically.

On May 25, 1979, a DC-10 carrying 272 passengers and crew crashed while taking off

WITNESS REPORT

O'HARE INTERNATIONAL AIRPORT TRAGEDY

Michael Laughlin, a pilot, was taking pictures of the airport as the disaster occurred.

After I had taken all the pictures I just stood there stunned, wondering to myself, "Did this really happen?"...I couldn't believe it. I just stood there shaking...

He explained what he saw when he first realized that the aircraft was having difficulty.

At about 60 meters [200 feet] off the ground the left engine seemed to explode away from the wing, although there was no smoke or flame. I saw the engine come tumbling through the air; tumbling and tumbling to the ground.

Source: *Chicago Tribune*, May 27, 1979.

ABOVE *Michael Laughlin's pictures of the DC-10 disaster were used by the* Chicago Tribune *newspaper.*

from O'Hare International Airport in Chicago. The crash happened because one of the airplane's engines fell off because of faulty maintenance work.

An even greater disaster happened on August 12, 1985. Shortly after taking off from Tokyo, the pilot of a Japan Airlines jumbo jet reported that he was having trouble controlling the airplane. It was losing height so he turned the aircraft around to return to Tokyo. But before he could reach the airport, the airplane went out of control and dived into the side of Mount Ogura to the northwest of the Japanese capital. Of the 524 people on board, only four survived. This is still the worst death toll for any

PILOT ERROR – THE M1 CRASH

Airline pilots are responsible for the safety of their passengers. They undergo a long period of training before they are allowed to fly an airplane, and they must have regular medical checkups to ensure that they are fit. Work schedules are arranged to minimize fatigue.

However, pilots do make mistakes despite being so well trained and cared for. Sometimes errors are made when pilots lose concentration, on long flights. Other mistakes occur when there is a sudden emergency and pilots make the wrong decision in the heat of the moment. This is what happened on January 8, 1989 to a Boeing 737 belonging to British Midland Airways.

single airplane disaster. The cause of the crash was the loss of the airplane's tail fin, which began to fall apart after takeoff. After a long investigation, Boeing, the manufacturers of the aircraft, admitted that repairs they had carried out on the Japan Airlines jumbo jet had been faulty.

ABOVE A victim of the Japan Airlines disaster is carried away on a stretcher ready to be flown to a hospital by helicopter.

LEFT A helicopter hovers over the site of the Japan Airlines crash, which happened on August 12, 1985. The airplane had crashed into a mountain near Tokyo and rescuers could not reach the scene of the crash on foot.

WITNESS REPORT

THE M1 DISASTER

A local man, Peter Wragg, witnessed the disaster.

We heard it approaching in the distance but this one was making a very strange booming noise like a very heavy backfire…a very frightening noise.

Once it drew level with the house you could see sheets of flame coming from one of the engines.

There was a great series of bangs and booming noises coming from the plane. The pilot was trying to get on the runway but hit the embankment.

Source: *Daily Express*, January 9, 1989.

A few minutes after takeoff from Heathrow airport, London, one of the airplane's engines suffered damage and loss of power. The pilot mistakenly ordered the wrong engine to be shut down and then diverted his airplane to land at East Midlands airport. When he started to fly towards the airport, the damaged engine suddenly lost all power. With no engines working, the airliner lost height rapidly and struck the ground in a field. It then bounced 230 feet to land on the M1 highway before plowing into an embankment. Forty-seven passengers died in the crash.

TOP *Using powerful lights to see by, rescuers work to free the trapped passengers from the British Midland Airways airplane that crashed on the evening of January 8, 1989.*

ABOVE *The wrecked Boeing 737 lying on the embankment of the M1 highway on the morning after it crashed.*

COLLISION!

The two points in an aircraft's flight when the risk of disaster is greatest are takeoff and landing. This is partly because the crew then have much more manual control of the aircraft than during the rest of the flight, when computers constantly check and correct the airplane's course, altitude, engine performance, and so on.

During takeoff and landing, it is important that the aircraft crew take their instructions from the air traffic controllers and carry them out exactly. The accident that took place in March 1977 at Los Rodeos airport (then called Santa Cruz), Tenerife, in the Canary Islands, shows how things can go disastrously wrong if these instructions are not obeyed.

Tenerife is a very popular island with vacationers, so Los Rodeos is a busy airport. On Sunday March 27, 1977, its one runway was even busier than usual. That morning, a terrorist bomb had exploded at Las Palmas airport on the neighboring island of Gran Canaria, and airplanes bound for Las Palmas had been diverted to land at Los Rodeos instead.

The first to arrive was a Dutch jumbo jet, KLM flight 4805, followed shortly by another jumbo jet, Pan Am flight 1736. Both pilots were instructed to park at the end of the runway to await permission to take off for Las Palmas. In all, there were eleven airplanes waiting at the airport, and only three air traffic controllers on duty.

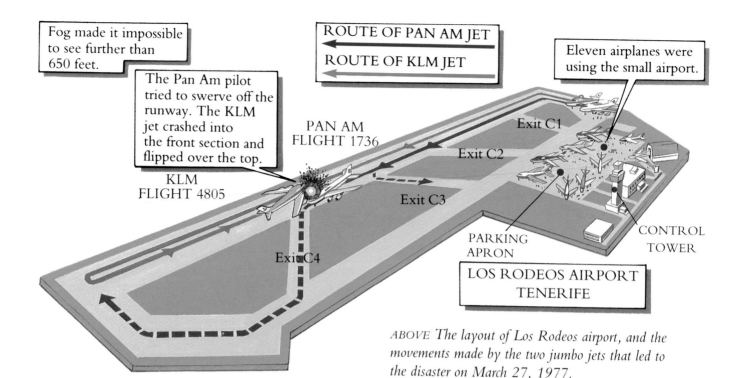

ROUTE OF PAN AM JET
ROUTE OF KLM JET

Fog made it impossible to see further than 650 feet.

The Pan Am pilot tried to swerve off the runway. The KLM jet crashed into the front section and flipped over the top.

Eleven airplanes were using the small airport.

PAN AM FLIGHT 1736

Exit C1

Exit C2

KLM FLIGHT 4805

Exit C3

Exit C4

PARKING APRON

CONTROL TOWER

LOS RODEOS AIRPORT TENERIFE

ABOVE The layout of Los Rodeos airport, and the movements made by the two jumbo jets that led to the disaster on March 27, 1977.

The KLM pilot decided to refuel his aircraft while he waited.

Meanwhile, an afternoon fog rolled down onto the airport, making it hard to see the runway. Finally, the KLM pilot was told to taxi his aircraft to the far end of the runway and await permission to take off. The Pan Am airplane followed some of the way before being ordered to leave the runway at exit C3. That was when the first mistake was made—the Pan Am pilot misunderstood and continued to taxi along the runway, heading for exit C4.

Then came a second error. The KLM pilot, who was unable to see the Pan Am jumbo jet in the fog, thought the runway was clear and began moving forward for takeoff. The Dutch airplane built up speed. When it had reached 180 mph., the Pan Am jet suddenly appeared out of the fog. The Pan Am pilot tried to swerve his airplane off the runway, but it was too late. The KLM jet struck the Pan Am craft at an angle of 45

degrees, its nose tearing into the roof of the cockpit and first-class compartment, while its massive engines smashed into the side. It then bounced over the Pan Am airplane and exploded on the runway beyond. A series of explosions ripped through the wrecked Pan Am jumbo jet and fires broke out. Survivors of the crash jumped for their lives and ran across the runway to safety. All the

WITNESS REPORT

LOS RODEOS DISASTER

An American vacationer, Jim Naik, was blown out of the Pan Am 747 by the blast and onto the runway.

I was in the first-class compartment and after the impact, people started just tumbling down from the lounge above on top of me.

Source: *Daily Express*, March 28, 1977.

passengers and crew aboard KLM 4805 were killed, and only 69 people escaped from Pan Am 1736. In all 583 people died, making this the worst aircraft disaster ever.

CATALOG OF ERRORS

These are the conversations between the pilots of the two jumbo jets—KLM 4805 and Pan Am 1736—and air traffic control (Control) leading up to the disaster at Los Rodeos airport.

Control: *Taxi into the runway and leave the runway third, third to your left, third.*
Pan Am: *Third to the left, OK.*
Control: *The third one to your left.*

This was where the first error occurred. Control wanted the Pan Am jumbo jet to take exit C3. Exit C3 was not normally used by jumbo jets. The pilot thought that Control meant him to take the third exit for jumbo jets, C4, which was farther along the runway.

KLM: *We are now ready for takeoff.*
Control: *OK, stand by for takeoff. I will call you.*
Pan Am: *Clipper 1736.*
Control: *Papa Alpha 1736, report runway cleared.*
Pan Am: *We'll report runway cleared.*
Control: *OK, thank you.*

This led to the second, disastrous, error. The KLM pilot heard Pan Am's conversation with Control, and thought it meant that the runway was already cleared. He may also have misheard Control's instruction to stand by for takeoff and believed he had been told simply to take off.

BELOW Investigators looking through the wreckage of the Pan Am and KLM airplanes.

SPACE – A DANGEROUS FRONTIER

Today, rockets carrying satellites and people into space are launched so frequently that some are not even reported in the news. Yet, as little as 40 years ago, space flight was only heard of in science fiction stories. This rapid change was possible because of two developments: engines that are powerful enough to push a rocket clear of the earth's gravity, and computers that can guide a spacecraft on its journey.

On April 12, 1981, the United States launched the first of a new type of spacecraft —the space shuttle. It consisted of a manned space-plane that was launched by two huge rocket boosters. After carrying out its mission in space, the shuttle could return to earth and be used again. Four shuttles were built: *Atlantis, Challenger, Columbia* (which flew the first mission), and *Discovery*. Between 1981 and 1986 they carried out a number of tasks in space, such as launching and repairing satellites, and performing experiments that could only be done outside the earth's gravity field.

On January 28, 1986 at the Kennedy Space Center, Florida, the crew of *Challenger* prepared for the launch of a mission, code-named STS 51-L. Just before 9:00 A.M., the seven astronauts took their places in the shuttle. The launch had already been put off several times because of technical problems. The crew expected it to be put off again because the weather was bitterly cold.

OPPOSITE *Seconds from disaster: the space shuttle* Challenger *lifts off from the Kennedy Space Center on January 28, 1986.*

THE *CHALLENGER* CREW
From left to right
Lieutenant Ellison Onizuka
  - *Air Force officer*
Commander Michael Smith
  - *Navy officer*
Christa McAuliffe - *Teacher*
Commander Dick Scobee
  - *Navy officer*
Greg Jarvis - *Engineer*
Judy Resnik - *Astronaut*
Ronald McNair - *Astronaut*

However, officials said that the launch would be able to go ahead in a few hours. At 11:15 A.M., it was definitely decided that the cold weather would not cause any problems and that the launch could go ahead. The final countdown began at 11:29, and *Challenger* lifted off on top of a column of flame at 11:38 A.M.

About 35 seconds later, as the rocket climbed high into the sky, it was hit by strong winds. The computers on board made continuous adjustments to make sure the shuttle stayed on course, and there was no sign of any danger. Then, when the shuttle had reached a height of about eight miles, the spectators at the launch site and millions of television viewers around the world watched in horror as a huge fireball engulfed the craft. The rocket boosters shot away in

THE *CHALLENGER* DISASTER

Christa McAuliffe was a teacher in New Hampshire when she was chosen from 11,000 people to be the first civilian astronaut. She received a lot of media attention and was often interviewed on television and for the newspapers. Before the disaster she was quoted as saying, "I still can't believe they are actually going to let me go up in the shuttle."

When asked if she was scared, she replied, "I wouldn't call myself a daredevil…I realize there is a risk…but it does not frighten me."

Source: *Daily Mail,* January 29, 1986.

ABOVE *Christa McAuliffe became a celebrity when she was chosen to be the first civilian astronaut.*

OPPOSITE *This picture was taken seconds after the explosion of the* Challenger *space shuttle.*

LEFT Challenger *was destroyed by an explosion in the left rocket booster.*

different directions and *Challenger* was hurled off course. Spinning violently at high speed and buffeted by strong winds, the craft was torn apart. All seven crew members died instantly.

WHAT WENT WRONG?

Scientists and engineers immediately began trying to find out what had gone wrong. When they studied the film of the launch, they noticed a small jet of flame coming from one of the joints in the casing of the left-hand rocket booster. The flame grew and started to touch one of the struts that connected the booster to the large fuel tank attached to the shuttle. A few seconds later, hydrogen began leaking from the fuel tank. Seventy-two seconds after lift-off, the hydrogen caught fire and the booster swung around. It punctured the fuel tank, causing a huge explosion. Although people knew what had happened, they still did not know why. Gradually the answer became clear. The rocket booster casing was made in sections that were joined together. Each joint was sealed with two circular rubber rings, called O-rings, which were held in place by the pressure of hot gases after the booster ignited.

However, on previous shuttle missions, the O-rings were found to have been worn away by the hot gases. What is more, tests had shown that the O-rings were much more likely to fail in freezing weather conditions. This is exactly what happened on the icy morning of the launch of mission STS 51-L.

The final question to be answered was why the mission was allowed to take place when it was known that there was a design flaw in the rocket boosters. The main reason was that the scientists and engineers who knew most about the shuttle and its operation did not have the final say about whether or not the launch should go ahead. That responsibility was given to the senior managers at the National Aeronautics and Space Administration (NASA). These people were influenced by the politicians who provided NASA with most of the money it needed, and by big businesses that hired the shuttle to launch their satellites and carry out experiments. Some people think that these interests were allowed to outweigh the scientists' fears that the rocket boosters were unsafe.

ABOVE *The next mission after the* Challenger *disaster was made by the* Discovery *space shuttle on September 29, 1988.*

OTHER SPACE DISASTERS

The *Challenger* disaster was not the first accident in which astronauts were killed. On January 27, 1967, three Americans died during the launch of the *Apollo I* mission. Then, on June 30, 1971, the three crew members of the Soviet craft

ABOVE The crew of the Apollo 1 mission during a practice session. All three died when their rocket caught fire as it was launched in January 1967.

Soyuz 11, who had earlier docked with an orbiting space station *Salyut 1,* were killed as they reentered the Earth's atmosphere on their return journey.

NASA has learned from the *Challenger* disaster. The design flaws have since been eliminated and scientists have been given more control of space missions. The shuttle program restarted on September 29, 1988, when the *Discovery* was launched and completed its mission successfully.

The *Challenger* shuttle disaster does not seem to have stopped people from wanting to explore space. However, it has helped slow down the headlong rush to explore it

as fast as possible. For complicated craft, such as the space shuttle, good, reliable technology takes a long time to develop, and the *Challenger* disaster showed that second-best is not good enough. The best technology also costs a vast amount of money to research and produce. The United States has found that its space program must be carried out more slowly if it is to be affordable both in terms of money and human lives.

TERRORISM IN THE SKIES

During the 1970s and 1980s, there were countless hijacks. Aircraft and passengers from Israel and other countries regarded as its allies, such as the United States and Britain, were especially targeted. This trend began in 1968, when a Palestinian group hijacked an Israeli airplane.

Two years later, three aircraft were hijacked and flown to an airport in Jordan and 300 passengers were taken hostage. The passengers were later released, but all three airplanes were blown up. From that time on, hijacking spread as other terrorists from other nations made contact with the Palestinian groups and were sometimes given training by them.

BLOWN OUT OF THE SKIES

One of the worst ever cases of airborne terrorism was not a hijack, but the planned destruction of a jumbo jet in flight. On June 23, 1985, Air India flight AI 182 was on its way from Toronto, Canada, to Heathrow airport in London, England. At 8:13 A.M., the airplane was 110 miles southwest of Cork, Ireland, flying at over 590 mph and at a height of about 31,170 feet. Suddenly, a bomb exploded in the forward (front) luggage hold; it had been smuggled on board inside a passenger's suitcase. The bomb blew a hole in the side of the airplane, which began to fall rapidly, falling apart as it plunged toward the sea. All 307 passengers and 22 crew died. The bomb had been

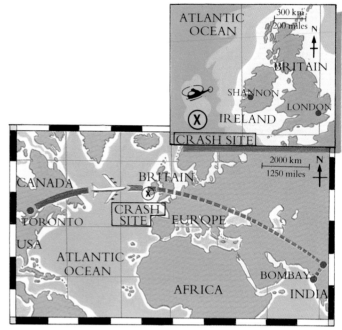

ABOVE MAP The route taken by Air India flight AI 182 and the position where the airplane crashed into the sea. BELOW A piece of the tail fin from Air India flight AI 182 floating in the sea near Ireland.

planted by Sikh terrorists who were demanding a separate Sikh state, independent from India.

26

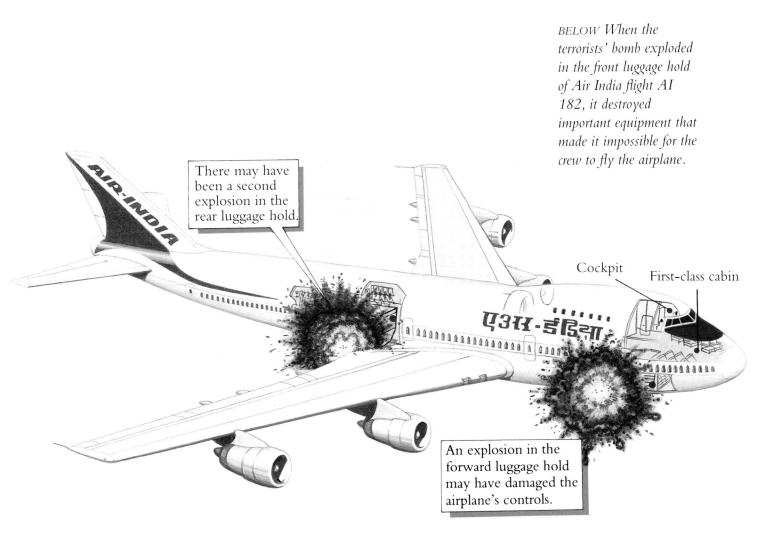

BELOW When the terrorists' bomb exploded in the front luggage hold of Air India flight AI 182, it destroyed important equipment that made it impossible for the crew to fly the airplane.

There may have been a second explosion in the rear luggage hold.

Cockpit

First-class cabin

An explosion in the forward luggage hold may have damaged the airplane's controls.

PAN AM FLIGHT 103 – *MAID OF THE SEAS*

Three years later, the world was shocked by another bomb that exploded on board a jumbo jet belonging to the American airline Pan Am. Flight PA 103 took off from Heathrow, London, at 6:25 P.M. on December 21, 1988, bound for New York. As it headed north the airplane was picked up on the air traffic control radar screens at

Prestwick, Scotland, and at 6:58 P.M. the pilot requested permission to turn westward.

The airplane, named *Maid of the Seas*, showed up on the radar screens as a small green cross inside a box. At 7:03 P.M. a controller at Prestwick watched in horror as the image on his screen changed. The single box representing PA 103 was suddenly replaced by five boxes, which stayed on the screen for a few seconds and then disappeared. Almost immediately, there were reports of an explosion on the ground.

Cockpit

Forward luggage hold

One cabin door found here.

Sixty bodies found here.

More bodies

One engine found here.

LOCKERBIE

Cockpit section fell here.

Both wings found here.

Fifty bodies found here.

More bodies

Three engines found here.

A74

ABOVE The wreckage of Pan Am flight PA 103 was scattered over a wide area in and around the Scottish town of Lockerbie.

The aircraft had broken up, and some large pieces had fallen on and around the Scottish town of Lockerbie. One of the wings, which was 48 feet long and contained about 24,000 gallons of fuel, crashed into a street and exploded. A huge fireball shot over 325 feet into the air, and flames engulfed a row of houses. The cockpit and first-class cabin smashed into a hillside overlooking the town. The main passenger cabin fell onto a house, chopping it in two; luckily, the occupant of the house survived. In all, 11 people in Lockerbie were killed by falling wreckage and fires. The death toll among those on board Pan Am flight PA 103 was much higher: none of the 243 passengers or 16 crew members survived. Smaller pieces of wreckage from the airplane were strewn along two trails,

WITNESS REPORT

Graham Byerley, who was staying in a hotel just outside Lockerbie, said:

We heard a rumbling…Then we looked out of the windows and could see sparks on the horizon and there was a tremendous bang…It was like a bomb going off or an earthquake. Then we saw an enormous fireball. The whole sky lit up and the ground was shaking.

Source: *Daily Mail*, December 22, 1988.

ABOVE *One of the houses that was destroyed by wreckage from the airplane.*

up to 80 miles long. Within a few days, tests carried out on the wreckage showed that the explosion on PA 103 had been caused by a bomb, probably containing a plastic explosive called Semtex. The bomb had been hidden inside a suitcase. An investigation revealed that the case containing the bomb had been put on board a flight in Frankfurt, Germany, which landed at Heathrow; passengers and luggage from the Frankfurt flight were then transferred to PA 103. Security checks at Frankfurt had failed to detect that the suitcase containing the bomb was checked in by someone who did not board the airplane to London. At Heathrow, the suitcase was simply moved from one airplane to the other.

BELOW *The cockpit and first-class cabin made up the largest single piece of wreckage, which landed on a hillside near the town.*

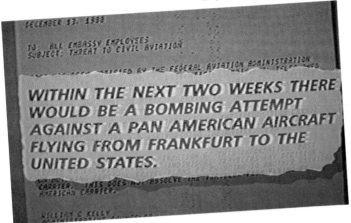

DECEMBER 13, 1988

TO: ALL EMBASSY EMPLOYEES
SUBJECT: THREAT TO CIVIL AVIATION

...SUPPLIED BY THE FEDERAL AVIATION ADMINISTRATION...

WITHIN THE NEXT TWO WEEKS THERE WOULD BE A BOMBING ATTEMPT AGAINST A PAN AMERICAN AIRCRAFT FLYING FROM FRANKFURT TO THE UNITED STATES.

CARRIER. THIS DOES NOT ABSOLVE THE...
AMERICAN CARRIER.

WILLIAM C KELLY

The suitcase was put in the *Maid of the Seas'* forward luggage hold. Just in front of this hold is a complex mass of electronic equipment, which controls the airplane's automatic pilot, radios, and navigation aids, along with the power supplies for all of the aircraft's systems. When the bomb exploded this equipment was destroyed, making the airplane impossible to fly. This is exactly what happened to the Air India jumbo in 1985, and the official report into that disaster recommended that jumbo jets be redesigned to strengthen the luggage hold and protect the important electronic equipment. This had not been done on the *Maid of the Seas*.

In theory, it is possible to make sure that terrorists cannot smuggle guns and bombs onto an aircraft. All luggage, including that belonging to the crew, is usually X-rayed, but it could be searched thoroughly by hand, as well. The passengers and crew themselves could also be searched, and then made to identify their own luggage before it is loaded. This would all take a good deal of time. Most airlines are unwilling to carry out all of these checks because they believe that passengers will not put up with the delays or the invasion of privacy that would result.

SEMTEX

The explosive Semtex can be molded into the shape of objects that do not appear suspicious, so it looks harmless when it passes through X-ray machines at airports. Also, it has almost no smell, making it hard to find using electronic "sniffing" equipment. In the case of PA 103, the Semtex bomb was hidden in a radio-cassette player. Even though this was X-rayed along with all the other luggage, the person whose job it was to operate the X-ray machine did not notice anything suspicious.

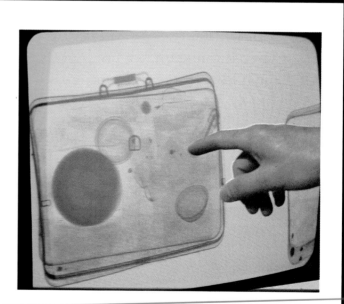

ABOVE A suitcase as it appears on the screen of an airport X-ray machine.

SHOT DOWN!

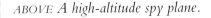

ABOVE *A high-altitude spy plane.*

LEFT *The cameras carried by a spy plane can produce very clear and detailed pictures of the areas they fly over. This is why the military forces in all countries are wary of unauthorized airplanes flying in their airspace.*

In the previous chapter, we saw how passenger aircraft can crash as a result of bombs planted by terrorists who want to gain publicity for their cause in a spectacular and gruesome way. But there have also been cases in which passenger aircraft have been blown out of the skies by the armed forces of hostile (enemy) countries.

The skies over a country are known as its airspace. Most countries guard their airspace very carefully because they fear attacks by military aircraft from other nations, or because they have secret military bases that they wish to keep hidden from spy planes. Airlines from any country always have to gain permission to fly through the airspace belonging to other countries, and they are given routes that must be followed exactly.

During the early 1980s, one of the countries that was more determined than most to protect its own airspace was the Soviet Union (U.S.S.R.). It was then one of the world's most powerful nations and had enormous armed forces. The country spent huge sums of money on military research and was dotted with top-secret installations.

One of the most sensitive areas of all was in the extreme east of the Soviet Union, consisting of the Kamchatka peninsula and the island of Sakhalin.

SHOOT NOW,
ASK QUESTIONS LATER!

On August 31, 1983, Korean Airlines jumbo jet flight KE 007 was on its way from Anchorage, Alaska, to Seoul, the capital of South Korea. About two and a half hours after takeoff, it strayed from its intended route and embarked on a course that would take it through Soviet airspace above Kamchatka and the island of Sakhalin. Six hours later, the airplane's captain sent his final radio message to an air traffic controller at Sapporo, Japan. He began, "This is KE 007…" but got no further. There was a sudden burst of noise on the radio, and then silence. The airplane continued to show on radar screens at Sapporo for several minutes before vanishing several miles west of Sakhalin.

When the news of the airplane's disappearance broke, there were several theories about what happened. Some people thought that a total electrical failure had caused the jumbo jet to crash, even though jumbo jets are known to have an extremely good safety record. The United States, however, was convinced that it knew the truth, and accused the Soviet Union of having shot down the Korean Airlines' jumbo jet, killing all 269 people on board.

The guessing continued for a week, until the Soviet Union finally announced that it had indeed shot down flight KE 007. The

BELOW The planned route of flight KE 007 and the course it actually flew.

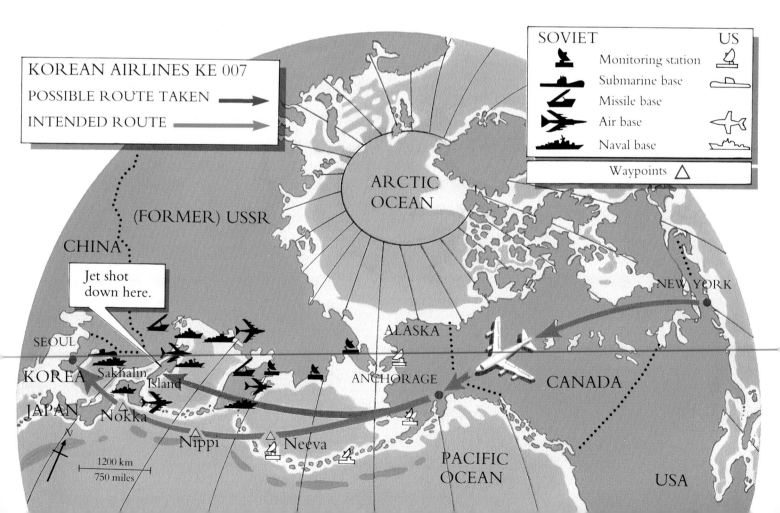

LEFT The families and friends of those killed on flight KE 007 protested in Washington, D.C., against the Soviet military attack on the civilian airliner.

BELOW A press conference at which representatives from the Soviet Union tried to explain why the Korean Airlines airplane was shot down.

Soviet government gave a variety of excuses for its actions, even blaming the United States by claiming it had sent the jumbo jet on a spy mission.

We will probably never know the exact details of what happened. However, we can piece together most of the story. As Korean Airlines' KE 007 flew over Kamchatka, it was detected by Soviet radar stations and fighter aircraft were launched. They were unable to find the jet, which passed over Kamchatka and headed for Sakhalin, where four more fighter aircraft were launched. Within ten minutes, one of the Soviet pilots announced that he had located the unidentified aircraft. From a distance of seven-and-a-half miles, he sent an IFF (Identify, Friend or Foe) message to the airplane, but received no response. He then closed to within one-and-a-quarter miles and fired two missiles. The fighter pilot reported to his ground control, "I have executed the launch; the target is destroyed."

Several important questions remain unanswered. One of these is why did flight KE 007 enter Soviet airspace in the first place? There were three separate navigational computers on board, and it is extremely unlikely that they could all have failed at the same time. Furthermore, why did the crew not realize the airplane was off

ABOVE *This is an artist's impression of the event that shocked the world, when Soviet fighter jets shot down a Korean Airlines airliner in August 1983.*

course and correct the airplane's direction? Along KE 007's intended route there are several "waypoints," and the crew had instructions to radio Sapporo Control in Japan and report when they passed each one. In fact, although they did give confirmation of their position at each waypoint, the image of the airplane on Sapporo's radar showed that by the time the crew confirmed reaching the final one, "Nokka," KE 007 was actually several hundred miles farther north.

One possible explanation is that the crew had flown its airplane off course intentionally, in order to make the journey shorter and save fuel. Korean Airlines' airplanes had certainly done this before, and one had even been forced to make an emergency landing when it was hit by gunfire from a Soviet fighter aircraft. It is still hard to believe that a pilot would take such a risk in a highly sensitive military area when he had almost 270 people on board. However, it is even harder to believe that the jumbo jet's navigation systems had not worked properly for six hours without the crew noticing.

The final question is why the Soviet fighter pilot was ordered to shoot down a passenger aircraft. The answer seems to be that the Soviet pilot thought he was attacking a spy plane and not a civilian aircraft. This is not quite as unlikely as it sounds because there was an American spy plane in the area at the same time. It had taken off from its base on Shemya Island, in the Aleutians, to listen in on Soviet communications from Kamchatka. At a

BELOW *A typical radar screen shows aircraft in flight as symbols or numbers. It would be difficult for an air traffic controller to know whether an unknown aircraft was a civilian airliner or a military spy plane.*

point near the coast of Kamchatka, its path crossed that of KE 007.

The Soviets were not surprised by the spy plane, because the United States flew similar missions on at least 20 nights each month. However, they were alarmed and confused to find not one but two large aircraft on their radar screens. Fearing that another hostile American airplane was in their airspace, the Soviets launched the first group of fighters from Kamchatka. When KE 007 was finally located, by the second group of fighters from Sakhalin, the attackers did not get closer than one-and-a-quarter miles to their target—which in the nighttime darkness would not have been close enough to make a positive identification. Their ground controllers appear to have panicked and given the order to fire without knowing for sure what the target was.

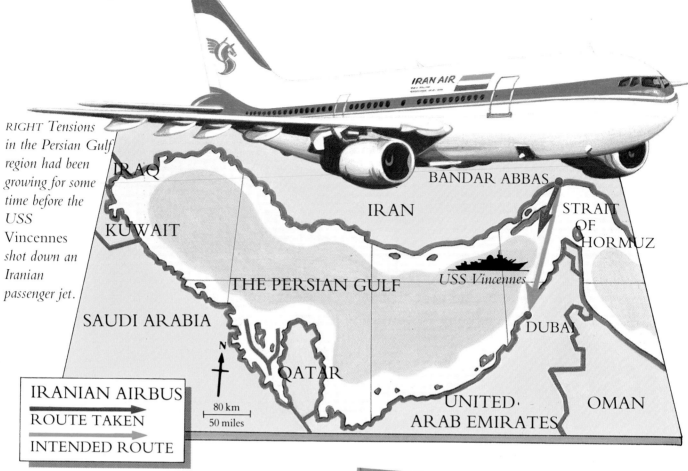

RIGHT Tensions in the Persian Gulf region had been growing for some time before the USS Vincennes shot down an Iranian passenger jet.

IRANIAN AIRBUS
ROUTE TAKEN
INTENDED ROUTE

80 km
50 miles

ANOTHER MISTAKEN IDENTITY

On July 3, 1988, another passenger aircraft was destroyed by military action. Radar operators aboard the American destroyer *Vincennes* reported a hostile enemy fighter in their area. Within minutes, the unidentified aircraft had been shot down. Sadly, it turned out that the "enemy fighter" was, in fact, an Iranian passenger aircraft with 290 people on board. There were no survivors.

The common factor linking the shooting down of both Korean Airlines' KE 007 and the Iranian airliner is that, in situations where there is a lot of tension, people are liable to panic and make wrong decisions. In both cases military personnel believed that they or their territories were about to be

ABOVE Some of the wreckage from the Iranian Airbus A300 aircraft shot down by the USS Vincennes.

attacked. In the heat of the moment, they wrongly identified passenger airplanes as military aircraft and shot them down.

AIR SHOW DISASTER

Air shows are extremely popular, and the biggest ones attract tens of thousands of people who come to see old and new aircraft going through their paces. The most spectacular events at these air shows are the demonstrations put on by teams of air force pilots flying high-speed military jets. They carry out complex and daring maneuvers in midair that often involve flying within a few feet of each other.

Because modern jets fly so fast, exhibition pilots have to be extremely skilled to avoid colliding with each other. Not surprisingly, there have been air-show accidents in which jets have crashed and their pilots been killed.

When this happens, the huge crowds that flock to see these displays are also at risk. In August 1988, at Ramstein in Germany, this risk turned to disaster.

A DANGEROUS SHOW

Crashes at air shows around the world are not uncommon. In Britain, for example, there were about 700 air shows each year between 1980 and 1992. Although most of these shows were very small, there were been more than 40 accidents and almost 30 deaths in that period. A number of exhibition pilots have also been killed in accidents during training. Between 1988 and

LEFT *Fabulous aerobatic displays, such as those put on by Britain's Red Arrows, draw huge crowds to air shows.*

This is the horrific sequence of events at the Ramstein Air Show on August 28, 1988.

TOP LEFT *Nine airplanes split into two groups: five swooped down to the left and four to the right. At about 200 feet from the ground they leveled out and flew through each other. The tenth airplane was supposed to race through the gap. Tragically, the pilot made an error and clipped the tails of two of the airplanes.*

MIDDLE LEFT *One of the airplanes burst into flames in midair and continued toward the crowd of spectators.*

MAIN PICTURE *The airplane crashed only feet away from the crowd and rolled over in a ball of flames.*

BOTTOM LEFT *The accident happened in seconds, so spectators had no time to avoid the burning wreckage.*

1992, Britain's Royal Air Force aerobatic team, the Red Arrows, lost six aircraft and one pilot in crashes during training.

RAMSTEIN AIR SHOW CRASH

On the afternoon of August 28, 1988, the air show at the United States air base in Ramstein, Germany, was nearing its end. The final act was being performed by the Italian Air Force team, the *Frecce Tricolori*. After a series of complex maneuvers, the ten pilots in their MB-339A jet trainer aircraft began the most spectacular part of their performance—a daring maneuver called *Arrow Through the Heart*. At its climax something went horribly wrong. One airplane clipped the tails of two others, causing all three jets to go out of control and crash. The aircraft that hit the other two had been flying straight toward the crowd. It plunged to the ground in front of them and exploded in a ball of flame, showering burning fuel and wreckage over the screaming spectators.

WITNESS REPORT

RAMSTEIN AIR SHOW HORROR

As the airplane that had been flying toward the spectators exploded, it threw blazing fuel and wreckage onto the crowd. Hundreds of people were injured. One of them described the scene:

We were caught in a rain of fire. There was just nowhere to run...I was burning. It was horrible...The flames got higher and higher. I don't know how I lived through it.

Source: *Daily Star*, August 29, 1988.

The fireball shot through the crowd, burning many of the people in its path. It also set fire to cars and trucks before burning itself out. A television cameraman from the West German station ARD said, "We saw the fireball racing toward us, so we first threw ourselves down on the ground." When the flames had died down, many people began searching for their friends and relatives, screaming their names. Others just stood still, too shocked to move. In all, 44 spectators and 3 pilots were killed, and more than 340 people were injured.

Is it possible to prevent similar disasters from occurring in future? The thing that makes air shows so popular is the very thing that also makes them dangerous—fast jets being flown with immense skill and precision in maneuvers that bring them to within feet of each other. The more

thrilling the maneuver, the less room there is for error and the greater the danger. The pilots who fly in air shows realize this, and know that their own lives are at risk. To combat this risk, they train and practice each maneuver until it is perfect. The three Italian pilots who were killed at Ramstein had a total of more than 9,000 hours flying experience. However, no matter how well trained they are, pilots are human and human beings can make mistakes. What changed the Ramstein crash from an accident involving three pilots into a disaster affecting hundreds of people was that the jets were close to the crowd when they collided, and that one airplane was flying toward the spectators. Since then, aerobatic teams have stepped up safety precautions. They now perform farther away from spectators and parallel to them, just in case another tragedy occurs.

ABOVE *The scene of the Farnborough Air Show disaster in 1952. One of the airplanes lost control and crashed into the spectators—29 people died.*

DANGER OF THE ELEMENTS

ABOVE *The tail section of the Air Florida airplane, which plunged into the frozen Potomac River near Washington, D.C., on January 13, 1982.*

In addition to all the other dangers that can lead to disaster, air travelers must also face hazards caused by the weather. On most flights, airplanes fly at altitudes well above storms, fog, and other weather-related dangers. However, when they are at lower altitudes—and especially during takeoff and landing—airplanes are vulnerable.

For this reason, aircraft are not normally permitted to take off in bad weather. If an airplane is heading for an airport that is shrouded in dense fog, covered in thick snow, or experiencing bad thunderstorms, it will usually be diverted to land at another airport where the weather is better.

Snow does not usually cause problems unless it falls so heavily that it settles on an airport runway faster than it can be cleared away. However, the events of January 13, 1982 at Washington National Airport, in Washington, D.C., show that even after an airplane has taken off, disaster can strike.

In the late afternoon, an Air Florida Boeing 737 waited for clearance to take off in the fierce blizzard that was sweeping over the United States capital. By the time the airplane roared along the runway, snow and ice had built up inside its engines. All modern passenger aircraft are fitted with engine deicers, but the Air Florida crew had not turned them on. As a result, the engines were not working efficiently and could not produce enough power to lift the airplane quickly. Ice had also built up on the aircraft's wings, adding to its weight and affecting the aerodynamic shape of the wings. Furthermore, the driving blizzard made it impossible for the crew to see where they were going. The combination of these three factors was especially critical, because Washington National Airport is located between two built-up areas, making it one of the most hazardous airports in the United States.

BELOW *Two rescuers searching for survivors or the bodies of victims from the Potomac River after the Air Florida crash.*

Shortly after it left the ground, the airplane nicked the south side of the 14th Street Bridge, which was crowded with rush-hour traffic crossing the Potomac River. The airliner pushed cars and their passengers from the bridge onto the frozen river and then "belly-flopped" into the icy water, making a gaping hole in the ice. Many of the people who fell into the river were paralyzed by shock and the cold water, and rescuers had to dive in to save as many as possible. Meanwhile, a helicopter hovered overhead dangling a lifeline for survivors to cling to while they were dragged to the shore. Some passengers could be seen still strapped into their seats and there were bodies lying on the bridge. When the rescue operation was completed, it was found that 78 people had died.

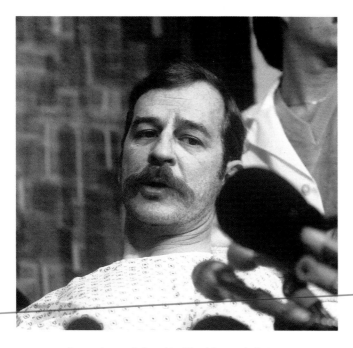

ABOVE *A survivor of the Air Florida crash being interviewed by reporters.*

The build-up of ice on the wings was also responsible for the crash of a Fokker F.28 of USAir on March 24, 1992, in which 27 people died. The airplane had just taken off from La Guardia Airport in New York, after being delayed for some time because of bad weather. During the wait for takeoff, snow was falling heavily and the airplane's wings had been sprayed several times with deicing chemicals. However, most of these chemicals only work for about 15 minutes, and the time between the airplane's last deicing and its takeoff was considerably longer than that.

CHILLING STATISTICS

In the 15 years prior to 1992, at least 20 jet airliners have crashed because of ice building up on their wings while they waited on the ground for takeoff. Crashes of this kind should not happen because they can easily be avoided by applying deicing chemicals to the wings. These deicers come in two forms—fluids, which take about 10 minutes to apply but are effective for only around 15 minutes; and gels, which work much longer but also take longer to apply to an aircraft. Fluids are much more widely used than gels.

ABOVE Part of the wrecked USAir Fokker F.28, which crashed after taking off from La Guardia Airport in New York.

LEFT *Deicing fluid is sprayed on to the tail of an aircraft waiting to take off in snowy weather.*

HELICOPTERS – FLYING AGAINST THE WIND

Airliners can fly above the weather, but helicopters operate at much lower levels. This means that they are more likely to fly in fog, snow, and high winds. Helicopters are often used to transport workers to and from offshore oil rigs. They are ideal for this task because they can take off and land vertically on a small heliport, whereas airplanes need a runway. However, in some offshore oilfields, weather conditions are often bad. This is especially true in the North Sea, off the north and east coasts of Britain.

On the night of March 14, 1992, the weather in the Brent oilfield, (62 miles northeast of the Shetland Islands), was violent. Winds of up to 60 mph were lashing the rigs and whipping up 40-foot waves in the sea. It was bitterly cold, and a snowstorm had reduced visibility almost to zero.

In these awful conditions, a *Puma* helicopter took off from the *Cormorant Alpha* oil production platform to transport 15 men to the living quarters on another platform. The two platforms were just 218 yards apart, although the pilot set out to fly in a wide, curved route lengthening the journey to about a half mile. The helicopter did not make it. After about 15 seconds it began to lose height and went into the sea about 100 yards from *Cormorant Alpha*. The crash was so sudden that the pilot did not have time to send a Mayday distress signal. Despite urgent

Crashes occur because airlines are anxious to ensure that their flights do not leave too far behind schedule. However, snow and ice inevitably slow down the rate at which airplanes can take off from and land at an airport. This means that, at busy airports, airplanes can be forced to wait for too long between deicing and takeoff—as happened at La Guardia in March 1992.

There are three possible solutions to this problem. Aircraft could be deiced closer to the point from which they take off. Alternatively, airlines could be forced to use deicing gels, which last longer than fluids. Finally, the number of aircraft using an airport affected by snow and ice could be cut to a figure that can be handled safely.

rescue attempts involving other helicopters searching with powerful floodlights, 10 passengers and the helicopter copilot died in the freezing waters. The pilot and 5 other men survived.

Immediately after the disaster, people asked why the helicopter had taken to the air in such appalling weather. Two days later, the team of accident investigators said that they believed mechanical failure had caused the crash and that they would be able to pin-point exactly what had gone wrong as soon as the flight recorder had been recovered from the seabed. However, when the flight recorder was found in the helicopter wreckage, nearly 400 feet below the surface, it showed that there had not been any mechanical breakdown. The pilot had simply been unable to control the small helicopter in such bad weather.

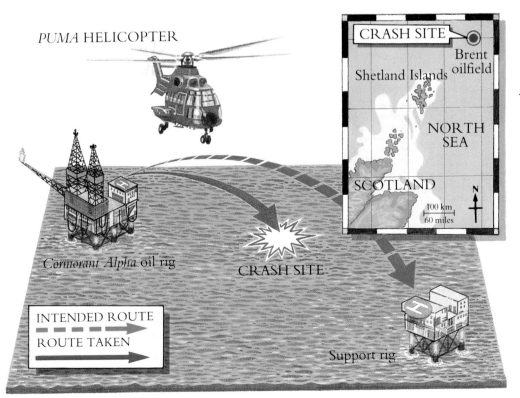

PUMA HELICOPTER

Cormorant Alpha oil rig

CRASH SITE

INTENDED ROUTE
ROUTE TAKEN

Support rig

CRASH SITE
Brent oilfield
Shetland Islands
NORTH SEA
SCOTLAND
100 km
60 miles
N

ABOVE *A helicopter takes off from the heliport of a North Sea oil rig. The North Sea is well known for its bad storms. Helicopters are very unstable during bad weather, but there is no other type of aircraft that can transport people or goods to the oil rigs.*

LEFT *The route taken by the* Puma *helicopter on the night of March 14, 1992. About 100 yards into the flight, the helicopter plunged into the sea.*

GLOSSARY

Aerodynamics   The study of how air moves over objects. Aircraft fly because of the special aerodynamic shape of their wings.

Air traffic controllers   The people who decide the direction, speed, and altitude at which airplanes may fly in a certain area. They give these instructions to aircraft pilots by radio.

Altitude   The height of something above sea level.

Automatic pilot   Sometimes shortened to "autopilot"; a device that automatically controls an airplane so that it will follow a planned course. The airplane's progress is constantly checked and any movement away from its intended course is corrected.

Aviation   Anything to do with flying.

Cockpit   The control area in an aircraft in which the crew sit while flying the airplane.

Diverted   To be changed from one route to another.

Electronic "sniffing" equipment   Special machines that can pick up the smells given off by explosive materials.

Glider   A winged aircraft without an engine. Gliders are pulled along the ground until their wings lift and launch them into the air.

Hijack   To seize an aircraft in flight by force and divert it from its course.

Jumbo jet   A name for any very large passenger aircraft, especially the Boeing 747.

Monoplane   An aircraft with a single pair of wings.

Mooring mast   A tall tower to which airships are attached before departure and on arrival at their destination.

Navigators   The members of a crew who plan the route that the aircraft should take.

Paralyzed   Unable to move part or all of your body.

Plastic explosive   A type of explosive that looks like jelly.

Pressurized cabins   The areas in an aircraft that have been built so that the air pressure is kept the same as at ground level. This means that the passengers and crew can breathe normally even at high altitudes.

Radar   Special equipment that can show the position of a large object on a screen by sending out radio wave signals.

Sabotage   To deliberately damage or destroy something.

Terrorist   A person or group who uses violence and fear to achieve an aim.

Taxi   When an airplane is moving away from or onto a runway.

FURTHER READING

Barrett, Norman. *The Picture World of Airport Rescue*. Picture World. New York: Franklin Watts, 1991.

Day, James. *The Hindenburg Tragedy*. Great Disasters. New York: Bookwright, 1989.

Horton, Madelyn. *The Lockerbie Airline Crash*. San Diego: Lucent Book, 1991.

Keller, David. *Great Disasters*. New York: Avon, 1990.

McCarter, James. *The Space Shuttle Disaster*. Great Disasters. New York: Bookwright, 1988.

Terror in the Skies: The Inside Story of the World's Worst Air Crashes. New York: Carol Publishing Group, 1988.

ACKNOWLEDGMENTS
Quote appearing on page 12: copyright © Macdonald Educational 1979. Reproduced by permission of Simon & Schuster Young Books, Hemel Hempstead, U.K.
Quotes appearing on pages 23 and 28: copyright © the Source/Solo.

PICTURE ACKNOWLEDGMENTS
Mary Evans Picture Library 5, 9(bottom); John Frost Historical Newspaper Service 12, 14(top); Impact Photos Ltd *cover* (background), 16 (both) (P. Gordon), 16(top); (J. Arthur) 29(top), (P. Cavendish) 29 (bottom); Photri 24, 25, 31(both), 35 (R. Nowitz); Popperfoto 4, 6, 10-11, 11(bottom), 40; Rex Features Ltd. *cover* (inset) (B. Arnaud), (Daifu) 14-15, (A. Shimbun) 15(top), (Alexandre) 19, 20, 30(top), (N. Jorgensen) 30 (bottom), (Trippett) 33(top) and 41, (Farnood) 36, 37, (B. Arnaud/G. Mannie) 38-39(all), 42 (Pereira), 43, 45; Frank Spooner Pictures (R. Faverty) 13, 17; Topham Picture Library 7(both), 8, 9(top), 21, 22, 23, 26, 33(bottom), 42(bottom), 44.
All illustrations are by Tony Jackson.

INDEX